Textiles and Ornaments of India

*The Trustees of the Museum of Modern Art wish to extend
their profound gratitude to the Government and the people
of India and to Their Excellencies Prime Minister
Jawaharlal Nehru, and the Ambassador from India to the
United States, G. H. M. Mehta, for the gracious attention and
assistance which enabled the Museum to prepare the exhibition
on which this book is based.*

William A. M. Burden, President

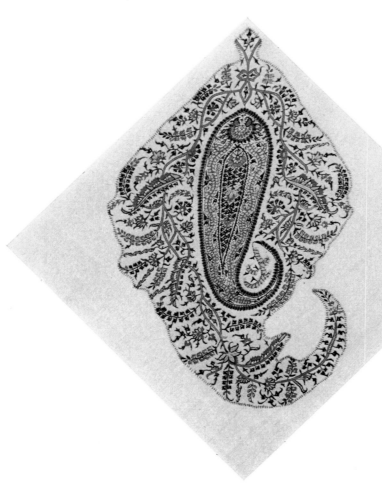

Detail of Kashmir shawl
19th century
Prince of Wales Museum of Western India, Bombay

Detail of silk-embroidered quilted cotton Kantha
East Bengal, mid-19th century
Private collection

Textiles and Ornaments of India

A SELECTION OF DESIGNS

EDITED, WITH A FOREWORD, BY MONROE WHEELER

TEXTS BY PUPUL JAYAKAR AND JOHN IRWIN

The Museum of Modern Art, New York

Acknowledgments

Sartorial and ornamental artistry being by its very nature a collective production, our thanks should first be given to the host of men and women of India whose rare talents produced the objects we have shown, and thereafter to the institutions and individuals named below for their gracious and invaluable coöperation. On behalf of the Trustees of the Museum of Modern Art I wish to express our profound gratitude to all those whose generous support, together with that of the lenders, made possible the exhibition recorded in this book. Particular thanks are due to Mr. Edgar Kaufmann, Jr., who assembled most of the material from which the exhibition was selected, and to Mr. Alexander Girard who devised the installation; to Sir Leigh Ashton, Director of the Victoria and Albert Museum in London, for the loan of hundreds of objects from its vast collections in this field; and to John Irwin, Assistant Keeper of the Indian Section, for his contribution to this book. Mrs. Pupul Jayakar, Special Deputy of the All India Handicrafts Board to the exhibition, provided counsel of inestimable value. Others who lent their gracious assistance were: Mr. Arthur S. Lall, Permanent Representative from India to the United Nations; Mrs. Kamaladevi Chattapadhyay, Chairman, All India Handicrafts Board, New Delhi; Professor Humayun Kabir, Secretary, Ministry of Education, Government of India, New Delhi; Mr. L. R. S. Singh, Consul-General of India in New York; Mr. W. G. Archer, Keeper, Indian Section, Victoria and Albert Museum, London; Dr. Maurice S. Dimand, Curator, Near Eastern Art, The Metropolitan Museum of Art, New York; Dr. Stella Kramrisch, The Graduate School of Arts and Sciences, Oriental Studies, University of Pennsylvania, Philadelphia; Dr. Moti Chandra, Director, Prince of Wales Museum of Western India, Bombay; Dr. A. I. Ghosh, Director General of Archaeology, Government of India, New Delhi; Mr. P. Neogy, Curator, Crafts Museum, New Delhi; Mrs. Sheila Bharat Ram, New Delhi; Miss Gira Sarabhai, Ahmedabad; Mrs. C. M. Bhimaya, Secretary, All India Handicrafts Board, New Delhi; Mrs. B. K. Nehru, New Delhi; Mr. L. C. Jain, General Secretary, The Indian Co-operative Union; Mr. K. R. Kripalani, Secretary to the Minister of Education, Government of India; Mr. Nityanand Kanungo, Deputy Minister for Village Industries, Government of India, New Delhi; Mr. Thomas B. Keehn, New Delhi Representative of the American International Association for Economic and Social Development; Mrs. Prem Bery, All India Handicrafts Board, New Delhi; the International Council of the Museum of Modern Art; Mr. Nelson A. Rockefeller; and the Rockefeller Brothers Fund.

The lenders to the exhibition were: Calico Museum of Textiles, Ahmedabad; Chicago Natural History Museum; Cleveland Museum of Art; The Cooper Union Museum for the Arts of Decoration; Crafts Museum, New Delhi; The Metropolitan Museum of Art, New York; Museum of Fine Arts, Boston; Prince of Wales Museum of Western India, Bombay; Textile Museum, Washington; Victoria and Albert Museum, London; All India Handicrafts Board, New Delhi; Mr. Charles Eames; Far Eastern Fabrics, Inc., New York; Mr. Alexander Girard; Mrs. Ruth R. Goddard; Mr. Tore Hakansson; The Heeramaneck Gallery; The Indian Co-operative Union, New Delhi; Mrs. Pupul Jayakar; Mr. Edgar Kaufmann, Jr.; Mr. Thomas B. Keehn; Mrs. Samuel A. Marx; Mr. Paul Mayen; Mr. and Mrs. Irwin Miller; Mrs. Marguerite Namara; Mrs. B. K. Nehru; Mrs. Dorothy Norman; Penthouse Gallery; Mrs. Sheila Bharat Ram; Mrs. John G. Rolph; Mrs. Manorama Sarabhai; Mrs. Donald Straus; Mr. Glenway Wescott; Mrs. L. B. Wescott.

The entire exhibition project was conceived and sponsored by the Museum of Modern Art's International Program, established in 1952 by the Rockefeller Brothers Fund. The International Council of the Museum of Modern Art made a generous gift of the color plates for this book.

Thanks are due to Mr. W. W. Hennessy for black and white and color photographs and also to Mr. Soichi Sunami for black and white photographs.

MONROE WHEELER, Director of the Exhibition

Contents

8

Photographs on pages 8, 9, and 10 were taken at the exhibition held in the Museum of Modern Art, 1955

Foreword

This publication—a picture book with interpretive essays—is based on an exhibition held at the Museum of Modern Art in the spring and summer of 1955.

Twenty-five years ago, to one visitor at least, the great sub-continent of India appeared to be mysteriously somnolent and indifferent to its ancient arts and architecture. By 1954, when this exhibition was conceived and assembled, the historic metamorphosis of independence had brought it all to life. Everywhere one heard enthusiastic expressions of the desire to improve living standards, to provide better education, and at the same time to revive the esthetic traditions and techniques of the great past. It is too soon to expect much new architecture, painting and sculpture, but in pride in the national heritage and in the all-important preservation of works of art, a renaissance is being prepared: the former viceroy's palace has been transformed into a National Museum, and there is a new National Museum of Modern Art.

Under the viceroys, the textiles and ornamental arts still persisted in traditional magnificence; but the deterioration and loss of techniques had begun with the introduction of Western industrial methods. Today, thanks to the imagination and determined effort of many men and women, with far-sighted government support, there is an attempt to stop the leveling and vulgarizing process and to preserve, in the inspired and painstaking handicrafts of the villages, the heritage of centuries past. One of the great textile concerns has established an excellent museum of traditional fabrics in Ahmedabad, and the government has founded a museum ot all the crafts in New Delhi. With funds derived from a tax upon manufactured goods, the state is supporting the All India Handicrafts Board and the Indian Co-operative Union, concerned extensively with the continuance of inherited techniques and the finest national designs.

There has always been a hierarchy in the arts; and of course the supreme creativity of India is to be found in its innumerable shrines and temples, with their fantastic profusion ot

sculpture, most of it an integral and immovable part of the buildings which it adorns; in the mysterious wall paintings in the caves at Ajanta; and in a wealth of exquisite miniature paintings.

But many a foreign traveler, when asked what has given him the most intense pleasure, will speak of the beauty of the multitudes of people in their fairy-tale raiment, of all colors of the rainbow, and in the brilliance and ingenuity of the ornaments worn with them. The splendor of the princely courts is proverbial all over the world, but in India the joyous love of color and the innate and almost unexceptionable taste of the women, even of the poorer classes, are no less impressive. Sometimes the workmanship and design of the inexpensive ornaments of the poor are as admirable as the gold filigrees of any rajah; and often a soapstone dish is a match for a jade vessel.

The great characteristic of Indian fine arts is that, in spite of virtuosity, the esthetic sense is always merged with the symbolic meaning. The same mentality seems to have preserved the modes of dress and decoration from much of the meretriciousness common in other cultures. As in the traditional dances where every gesture is equivalent to a word or a concept of myth or faith, every color, every woven or printed pattern, every necklace, bracelet or tinkling anklet means something to the wearer.

The extravagant and unforgettable colors at first seem to clash before occidental eyes, but they soon assert surprising harmonies. In addition to their richly-hued saris, the women are laden with elaborately worked metals, minerals, glass. Even the ubiquitous cattle, and the camels and elephants, are adorned and painted. At the festival called "Holi," people throw powdered bright pigment upon one another, half in farce, half in magic. But here, too, the mood is not materialistic or entirely frivolous. Uppermost in the mind is the close connection, indeed identification, between the brief and elemental human fate and the godhead. Toys of perishable and gaily painted clay and wood are in fact ritual offerings of solemn import. Intricate workmanship of paper or the pith of palm trees is for a moment's festivity, but of the spirit.

All this symbolism and playfulness, flamboyance and poverty, is India—and when the Museum came to consider how it should be shown, India itself, appropriately, gave guidance and a prototype. The presentation devised and installed by Alexander Girard was given the form of an imaginary bazaar or market place. Twelve square gilt columns were set around a fifty-foot pool of water and reflected in a wall of mirror at one end. Over the water were hung informally a bewildering assortment of saris, intricately woven silks and simple but vigorously designed muslins, and dotted tie-dyed turban cloths—a vast palette of crimson, dark red, yellow, moss green, purple and sky-blue—many profusely threaded with gold, as though with sunshine. Near this, the rarest brocades, tinseled gauzes, gossamer cottons and Kashmir shawls were ranged, and on other walls were temple cloths, carpets and embroideries. In an adjacent room, under a patchwork canopy, and beside a window adorned with paper kites, glittered a treasure-trove of the work of jewelers, goldsmiths, silversmiths and jade-carvers: precious stones strung as prodigally as beads; mere glass in miraculous settings; and fire-bright enamels of the sixteenth and seventeenth centuries. Another room was devoted to a great variety of tribal attire, household utensils, ritual figures, vessels of iron inlaid with silver, boxes and pouches, trays and baskets, toys and bouquets of paper flowers.

The enthusiasm generated by the exhibition in the minds of hundreds of thousands of Americans prompted the Museum's Junior Council to present in the auditorium a series of six evening performances called *The Living Arts of India,* consisting of the first appearance in America of the Indian musicians, Ali Akbar Khan (sarod), Chattur Lal (tabla); the classical dancer, Shanta Rao; and the world première of Satyajit Ray's film "The Story of Apu and Durja." These special events were made possible by the support of the Government of India, the Ford Foundation TV Workshop, Hemisphere Films, Inc., Yehudi Menuhin and the Junior Council Committee under the guidance of Ann C. Resor and Elizabeth Sprague Smith.

Special acknowledgment to those who enabled us to present our survey of the great crafts of India to the American public will be found on page 6. —M.W.

The Seasons

SUMMER *In the hot breathless summer, maidens shed their lime green veils*
from masses of dark hair, from quivering shoulders.
And now, they apply sandal paste to their breasts and cover them with transparent cloths,
with jasmine, and snow white pearls.
At night, moon bright terraces are fragrant with the breath and lips of sleeping women.

THE RAINY SEASON *In the season of rains, rivers surge to embrace the sea.*
And maidens loosen their hair and place yellow blossoms behind their ears.
Pearl necklaces cling to swelling breasts. Young girls wear garments of white about the hips.
The bride, perfumed with sandal paste and incense,
hearing the roar of rain-laden clouds, shyly seeks her bridal chamber.

THE AUTUMN *Autumn comes, and the skies are clear of rain and gentle breezes stir the moon lotus.*
Maidens decorate their hair, dark like a cloud of rain, with the jasmine flower,
and place buds of the indigo lily behind their ears.

THE SEASON OF FROST *The falling dew brings with it the season of frost.*
Fields are mellow and fruitful with grain and mouths are moist with flower-fragrant wine.
Women of fashion use perfumed powders and wrap their bodies in heavy silks,
and in their hair is incense smoke. The young pouting maiden, mirror in hand,
her eyes red with her wakeful night of love,
makes up her lovely face, in the light of the morning sun.

THE WINTER *When winter comes, robes lie heavy upon swelling hips*
and women hide their breasts in light bodices,
for the time of fragrant sandal paste cooled by moonbeams has passed away.
There are no jeweled belts, no chains, no anklets
that vie with the song of birds, on feet that are as lilies.
And now women's bodies are golden with the fragrance of saffron and musk.

SPRING *With spring the heart awakens to new rhythms and life quickens in the mango trees.*
The palasa flowers burst into bloom, fire-red like a parrot's beak.
Pearls linger on rounded breasts, trembling under the movement of perfumed breaths.
Hips are impatient of golden chains. Maidens wear silk garments dyed yellow
or red with the juice of the Kusembha flowers, and on their breasts are tissues stained ochre brown.
In their garments are woven bright flamingoes.
In spring, the bodiless love-god enters the limbs of maidens.

After Rinisamhara of Kalidàs, 5th century, A.D.   by Pupul Jayakar, with acknowledgments to Ranjit. S. Pandit

The dancer Shanta Rao in South Indian costume
Color photograph by Herbert Matter

Cotton hanging, showing Persian influence.
Depicts angels dancing and playing
musical instruments in a forested paradise.
Hand-stenciled and painted, 27 x 32½″
Masu lipatam, 17th century
The Heeramaneck Gallery, New York

Indian Fabrics in Indian Life

BY PUPUL JAYAKAR

To discover the sources of their inspiration and to comprehend the inherent significance of the vast field of Indian fabrics, they should be seen in context, against the social and historical background from which they have emerged and on the dark-toned bodies of the people for whom they were made. For in India, textiles have rarely been concerned with fashion or individual separateness and uniqueness; rather, garments have always been only one part of a complex ritual of life, one aspect of a preordained milieu in which man is born, grows to stature, and dies.

The response to form and texture, the total attitude toward dress, were dictated by forces unanswerable and unalterable, and were a projection of group sensitivity and awareness, the outcome of endless generations of unconscious creative impulse rather than a manifestation of contemporary or individual response to environment or events.

Innumerable invasions of virile, nomadic peoples migrated over the length of India: vast civilizations intermingled. Alien myths, ancient gods, and cults of the original inhabitants of this land; the topography of mountains, deserts and lush vegetation, and the presence of minerals, salts and water, all were factors that molded the esthetic expressions. A people rose, nurtured by profound theories of life, visualizing the universe and time as rising from chaos through millenniums, to sink back again into chaos, then to re-emerge, contracting and expanding, until yesterday and tomorrow were telescoped in this continuum.

It was against this field that hereditary guilds evolved, organized within rigid caste systems and protected by rigid caste laws. Tracing guild origins back to *Visvakarma,* the very source of creative intellect, the craftsman combined within his being the functions of both receiver and executor. He became in society the symbol, the outer manifestation, of creative purpose. The integration of creative endeavours with livelihood, the refusal to permit outside influences to permeate and corrupt the unconscious process of renewal, led to the great long flowering of the craft tradition in India. The craftsman was the link in an unbroken tradition which embraced both producer and consumer within a social–religious community. Art and esthetics were deeply rooted in function.

With an extensive tradition of myth, symbol, and fantastically rich imagery, there was no place for stagnation in the Indian textile crafts, for although forms were repeated, they were free from imitative intention, and each productive act was spontaneously linked with the stream of man's life, a dynamic symbol of man's endeavour to express universal human emotions and interests.

Different forms existed from the earliest times in garments, headdresses, shoes, jewelry. Each ethnic group maintained separate characteristics which became symbols of recognition and identification and served to establish common ancestry. To this day in Gujarat, Kathiawar and Rajasthan, women of the cowherds, the camel drivers, the Bhils, the nomad Gurajars, wear costumes of flared skirt, bodice and head-cloths made from resist-dyed fabrics, each group displaying totally distinct motifs and colors. Even the arrangement of patterns on these cloths is so distinctive that identification is relatively simple.

There is no record of a time when the people of India did not grow cotton, weave and dye cotton cloth, and wear patterned cotton garments. A fragment of a madder-dyed cotton cloth has been found at Mohenjo-Daro, establishing knowledge of cotton weaving and of the fabulous process of mordant dyeing five thousand years ago. There are indications that silk and woolen cloths were also known from very early time.

There are records of the export of silk and cloth of gold to Rome in the reign of Tiberius. But the knowledge of silk weaving is known to have come from China, and the Sanskrit word for silk cloth is closely linked with its Chinese origin. It was in cotton that the genius of the Indian weaver, printer and embroiderer was to find its richest and boldest expression.

The manner in which this genius expressed itself was determined by the configuration of the land itself. In the West, we find a great belt stretching from Sind to Baluchistan through Kathiawar and Rajasthan to Gujarat, where the bare stretches of sand, the intolerable heat of the noonday sun, and the fantastic twisted forms of cactus and the thorny babul tree, demand compensation in the deep glowing colors of the resist- and tie-dyed cloths of this area. As we go further south into the hilly tracts of the Deccan, formal patterns grow in importance, colors lose their superlative brilliance and become darker and more subdued, till they quench themselves in the lush forests of the backwaters of Malabar. Here the color of the natural background prevails and garments divest themselves of pigment as a relief from the fantastic colors of sky, water and trees.

Above: Detail of cotton block print
Bombay, 20th century
All India Handicrafts Board, New Delhi
Below: Detail of cotton tie-dyed sari
Rajasthan, 20th century
All India Handicrafts Board, New Delhi

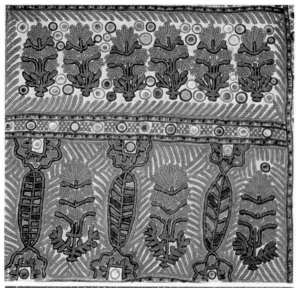

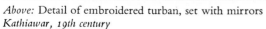

Above: Detail of embroidered turban, set with mirrors
Kathiawar, 19th century
The Calico Museum of Textiles, Ahmedabad
Below: Detail of silk tie-dyed sari
Kathiawar, 20th century
The Calico Museum of Textiles, Ahmedabad

Above: Detail of embroidered silk skirt
Cutch, 19th century
Victoria and Albert Museum, London
Below: Detail of silk brocade shawl
Chanderi, 18th century
The Calico Museum of Textiles, Ahmedabad

On the east coast extends a great weaving belt, from Assam through Bengal, Bihar and Orissa, Andhra and Tamilnad. Right up to the end of the nineteenth century cotton hand weaves were produced in parts of this area, the like of which have not been seen in the world. Those from Dacca were known as *mulmul khas* or King's muslin and bore names like *bafthawa*—woven air, and *shabna*—morning dew.

The emphasis in these regions was on pattern and form; motifs of rare elegance and sophistication emerged with startling clarity directly from the weaving technique. Colors disappeared into the background and became in a manner incidental to pattern and texture.

With the establishment of Aryan supremacy, and the splitting of the social structure into conqueror and conquered, the Aryan and the Dasyus, there developed a craft tradition which flourished for over three thousand years. The invasions that stormed India subsequent to the Aryans only strengthened this development by widening the distance between the ruler and his court, and the people. The conquerors introduced new art forms and concepts, new garments and symbols; the challenges of various esthetic viewpoints were accepted by the craftsmen and absorbed and assimilated. So long as the patrons were men of exceptional sensitivity, the forms that emerged bore evidence of this, but as the taste of the master degenerated, the vision of the craftsman dimmed, and clarity of form disappeared. Techniques sometimes improved, but the living element that gave value to the technique died, leaving a stagnant craft.

Two channels of craft expression developed from the start. The one was concerned with surface treatment reflecting as in a mirror the prevailing culture patterns of the patrons and responding to every sophistication and rare elegance. The other was structural in concept, rooted in the earth, reflecting the familiar forms of the unchanging village unit, the romance and emotional background of nomadic tribes, the rituals that bound man with invisible chains to his ancestors.

Nearchus, writing in the third century B.C. of the court of Chandragupta Maurya, mentions Indians wearing "linen of trees" (cotton) shining white against the darkness of their skins. He speaks of tunics worn ankle length, of two pieces of stuff, one thrown over the shoulder, the other wrapped around the head; also of men who wore earrings and dyed their beards crimson, white, blue-black and green, who wore shoes of white leather elaborately worked, with variegated high heels. This dress is as alien to the garments found on the Mauryan terra cottas of that period, as the fabrics worn today by rural women in some distant village of Rajasthan are to the saris worn at the race courses of Bombay or Calcutta. These two kinds of design expression have always coexisted in India.

The village textile tradition, rooted in custom and ritual, was based on a deep comprehension of the nature of mass and volume in which depth of color was a vital dimension. The processes of resist-dyeing, tie-dyeing, and yarns tie-dyed to a pattern before weaving were the basic techniques of indigenous village cloths. *Al* root or lac was used for the reds, indigo for the blues, iron shavings and vinegar for the blacks, turmeric for the yellows and pomegranate rind for the greens. Color was not a pigment applied to the surface, it so permeated the fabric that it became an integral part of the material. A superlative knowledge of color chemistry and of the rich resources of madder dyeing gave to India's colored cloths a quality of growth and maturing, in which the colors ripened in the sun. The sun was a catalytic agent which constantly acted and reacted upon the minerals, vegetables and water, so that color came to life in response to the sun's rays; the fading too was like flowers that age in the sun, giving back their color to the energy that gave it birth. Fading was a graceful process of soft tones unutterably beautiful against the dark skins of the women, the red and ochre colors of the earth and the green fields of a countryside; in this process no cloth looked drab or ugly but only grew older with the body of the person who wore it.

Sensitivity to color has expressed itself in most of the romantic folk poetry and ballads of India. Colors were surcharged with emotional content and rich association. Red was the color of the *Chunari,* a tie-dyed sari, and was the symbol of *sohog,* the first days of marriage and love play. It was the garment worn by the *Abhisarika,* the young woman seeking in the darkness of night her waiting beloved. Saffron or *gerua* was the color of *Vasant,* of spring, of young mango blossoms, of swarms of bees, of southern winds and the passionate cry of mating birds. Maroon and black were the colors of mourning. Blue or *nil,* the color of indigo, was also the color of Krishna, the cowherd child-god who bore the name of *Navjaldhar*—he that is of that color, that of the newly formed cloud, dormant with the darkness that is rain. But there was another blue, *Hari nil,* or the color of water in which is reflected a clear spring sky. Even the great gods had their individual colors: Brahman was red, Shiva was white and Vishnu was blue.

These colors, when worn by peasant or householder were but a projection of the colors and cloths worn by the god enshrined in the temple, and formed another link between man and his God. As there were musical *rāgas* and *rāginis* (modes or melodic forms) suited to every movement of the changing seasons, and to express every shade of human emotion, so each musical tone had a dominant color from its presiding deity; colors when worn by men and by the enshrined godhead reflected not only every movement of the stars in the heavens, but were indications of moods and emotions evoked by the changing seasons. This expression of moods through color and dress was considered of such consequence that special garments were prescribed for a love-sick person, for a repentant person and for persons observing vows.

Pattern in traditional village cloths, although vigorous and vital in its elemental simplicity and absence of unessential detail, was subordinate to color. Pattern broke up the color mass, enhancing its interest, it was used to relieve monotony but rarely as the focal point. The decorative motifs were geometric and highly stylized. Rings, dots and zig-zag ornaments were used within panels, arranged both horizontally and vertically. Symbols were clearly defined and tended to develop towards total abstraction. They were drawn from and portrayed the background of village life. New elements, as they entered the consciousness of the village artisan, were translated by him into abstract symbols with the same clear elemental concepts of structure and form. I have seen airplanes, clocks and gramophones used as motifs to ornament village clothes without the cloth losing its essential quality.

Religious tradition was the very core of village textile design. Temples claimed for their rituals the finest creations of the craftsmen. Only the perfect-without-blemish could be offered to the godhead. To satisfy this demand, craft schools sprang up around the main religious centers, fulfilling the needs of the temple and of the pilgrims who thronged there. Among the richest expressions of this tradition were the temple cloths made in many centers in South India, Gujarat and Rajasthan until the beginning of the twentieth century. These temple cloths were an extension of the fresco or mural tradition. They illustrated episodes from the Ramayana, Mahabharata and the Puranic legends and myths. Temple cloths were hung on the walls of inner shrines and decorated the wooden temple cars of the god when he was taken out in procession. Religious ritual did not confine itself to the place of worship; it extended to and enfolded the daily life of the householder. No garment ever was completely secular. The dress worn by the young girl, by the bride, by the young woman carrying her first unborn child, the dress of the woman in mourning, or in widowhood, and the cloth which covered her body after death, were all prescribed and dictated by the demands of ritual. The unbleached, unsewn garment worn by the woman as a *sari* or *dupatta* and by the man as *dhoti,* shawl, or as a turban around his head, was emblematic of unsullied purity and was imbued with magical properties. The Gujarat bride wore the unbleached ivory-toned cloth at the time of her marriage, and the householder shed his upper, sewn garments to wear it at the time of worship. Silk, dyed a deep gold yellow or glowing vermilion, known as *pitamber* was prescribed for certain ceremonies. Moslems were forbidden the use of pure silk; the half-cotton, half-silk fabrics, known as Mashru and Himru, were a response to this taboo.

The court tradition, based as it was on the changing demands of rulers and reflecting within its creative expression every accent of the sensitivity or degeneration of its patrons, became established early in the history of Indian textiles. It found its richest expression within the great craft schools which sprang up around the Mogul courts at Delhi and the Imperial courts of Golconda. Miniatures of the period reveal extraordinary beauty and richness of texture and pattern in the fabrics worn by the kings and their courtiers. Heavy gold cloth was often used for end pieces on the rarest muslins which were of such inconceivable fineness that they were said to become invisible when moistened and laid on the grass. As the goldsmith fashioned the beaten sheet of gold and enameled glowing spots of color into it, so the painter, weaver or embroiderer used his skill to bring to life glowing jewel-like ornaments on the heavy gold end pieces of the *patkas* and the *dupattas*. If the inspiration of the village cloths was a concept of mass and volume, these court fabrics were expressions of an exquisite and highly cultivated knowledge of line. In the one, textile design expression was concerned with relief within the mass; the other, with creating clear accents against a neutral background. The one produced an effect of a relief in red sandstone, the other the effect of marble inlay. The indigenous name for these court cloths was *minakar,* that is to say, enameled.

Thus the treatment of pattern in these cloths was linear rather than structural. Floral motifs were most commonly used and were spaced across the length of a cloth. The great love the Moguls had for flowers and gardens inspired many of the cloths of their period. These floral motifs were shaded in various tones of madder red to produce effects of great delicacy and beauty.

Export trade projected the court tradition into a wider field. In the court it was the king, the main patron who prescribed the trend; in trade, it was the distant consumer who dictated. In both cases, the producer was subordinate to the consumer's demand.

Trade in cotton cloth is known to have existed between India and Babylon from before the time of Buddha, twenty-five centuries ago. Silk and gold cloth were carried by traders known as "merchants in blue cloth and broidered work."

Trade was of such importance that whole villages sprang up solely occupied with producing and processing cloth for a foreign market. To this day there is a village in Gujarat called Pithapur where blocks for printing are cut chiefly for the manufacture of *soudagir* or trade cloths for export. And at Benares, Farokhabad, Kashmir and Lucknow there are large groups of hereditary craftsmen who work solely to produce weaves, prints and embroideries to satisfy foreign demands. The skill of the Indian craftsman makes it simple for him to adapt his technique to new forms. Many of the cloths produced for a foreign market show no trace of the traditional designs and motifs of India. Indigo-dyed fragments of Indian muslin which have patterns directly adapted from Arabic motifs have been found in Egyptian tombs. This has made it difficult to identify many Indian cloths that have survived in other parts of the world.

Most of the so-called Indian cloth commonly found in Europe and America and associated with India has little link with the textures and designs of the fabrics worn by the Indian peoples. And unfortunately, much of the existent literature on Indian textiles deals with these trade fabrics, forgetting that they are but one manifestation of a craft tradition. There has been a tendency to base whole theories about Indian textiles on this one-sided source material.

In this short essay I have attempted to clarify the structure of Indian textile design and to indicate the various means through which a great craft tradition has attempted to express itself. Without a comprehension of this background it is difficult to associate or assess a Benares gold woven scarf and a resist-dyed cloth of Rajasthan. For between the two lies a vast gulf, not only of costliness, but of attitude and consciousness.

Within the last generation there has been a rapid transformation in the social structure of India. The building of roads, the introduction of machines, the breakdown of caste barriers, the carrying of an urban civilization through radio and cinema to the doorsteps of rural communities, has led to a rapid breakdown of the norms that had directed craft traditions. Today it is the town that is dictating the fashions of the village and in most village fairs the cloths that are sold are no longer resist- or tie-dyed cloths produced by local craftsmen, but the latest patterns woven in a local textile mill.

The snapping of the link between the creative impulse and livelihood is the inevitable outcome of mechanization. The introduction of an alien concept of the designer as distinct from the craftsman has only further destroyed the craftsman's natural response to good form. This has led to increasing tensions in the craft tradition and a confusion of the unconscious background that is the very source of the creative process. That it has happened accidentally and not from a conscious awareness of the situation has only tended to produce greater chaos. The Indian craftsman is faced with a situation where, on one side, he is admonished to turn "back to the past" and, on the other, he is dazzled by incomprehensible forms evolved in the West after centuries of experimentation. To go back to the past is impossible, for the past was background to a life that has no longer any meaning in terms of the new social order. The mere absorption of Western forms equally has no meaning, for they are alien and have no link with the craftsman's comprehensions and concepts. What then is possible? The question has no easy solution. It may well be that the very laying bare of the problem with all its intricacies, conflicts and tensions will in itself project the answer. No single human mind can mold the unconscious impulses of a craft tradition; it can only help cleanse the eye of the craftsman of the corrupt forms that have blurred his vision, and allow the incredible creative force that still lies deeply embedded within his eyes and hands to discern and create a new tradition of textile design for the India of today and of the future.

Main Processes of the Dyed Fabrics of India

BLOCK PRINTING, in which the design is cut in wood, and stamped in color on the cloth.

RESIST-DYEING, in which parts of the cloth are treated with a substance which prevents the cloth from absorbing the dye.

MORDANT-DYEING, in which the design is applied to the cloth in chemicals which, when immersed in other chemicals, bring out the desired color.

TIE-DYEING, in which portions of the cloth not to be colored are plucked up in the fingernails of the maker and wound many times with waxed or starched string, and then immersed in the dye which does not penetrate the tied parts. Beginning with the lightest color, this process is repeated one or more times, according to the design.

IKAT, a variant of tie-dyeing in which, before the cloth is woven, portions of the individual threads are colored at carefully measured distances, so that as the weaving proceeds the final design appears.

Indian Textiles in Historical Perspective

BY JOHN IRWIN

In India, the decorative arts reflect something fundamental in the traditional way of life: certainly more than the mere wish to be gay and sociable. No one who has been among the colorful crowd in Indian villages and market towns can ignore this impression. Costume and jewelry are not the only clues. It is expressed in the way even the poorest farmer will find a fitting moment to ornament his bullock's horns with silk tassels, and in the ubiquity of the flower-garland as a symbol of dedication. India is perhaps the only country in the modern world to support a large profession of garland-makers.

The spontaneity and instinctive good taste which characterize the old way of life cannot, of course, be considered apart from the tradition of handicraft on which it is based. Accustomed as we are to a sentimental view of handicraft as a reaction from mechanization, we must remember that in India this tradition survives—however precariously—in its own right. We are too late to stem the tide of mechanization; but we still have time to develop a better understanding of the way of life the handicraft represents.

The Western industrial designer who caters to metropolitan fashion and is the self-conscious creator of designs he regards as his own, has no real counterpart in handicraft tradition. In the latter, tradition and convention are binding; habit, rather than self-consciousness, governs the approach. This is not to say that designs were static: only that changes were slower and more akin to growth, as even swift observation of the modern and historical textiles of India in this book will show.

For two thousand years or more, Indian history has been closely bound up with her pre-eminence as a producer of textiles. Imagery of the loom is a feature of her poetic tradition. In the sacred *Vedas,* Day and Night are said to spread light and darkness over the earth as weavers throw a shuttle on the loom. In other parts of the ancient world as well, Indian fabrics were proverbial. As early as 200 B.C. the Romans used a Sanskrit word for cotton (Latin *carbasina,* from Sanskrit *karpasa*). In Nero's reign, delicately translucent Indian muslins were fashionable in Rome under such names as *nebula* and *venti textiles* (woven winds), the latter exactly translating the technical name of a special type of muslin woven in Bengal up to the modern period. The *Periplus Maris Erythraei,* a well-known Roman document of Indo-European commerce, gives to the main areas of textile manufacture in India the same locations as we would find in a nineteenth-century gazetteer and attributes to each the same articles of specialization. The quality of Indian dyeing, too, was proverbial in the Roman world, as we know from a reference in St. Jerome's fourth-century Latin translation of the Bible, Job being made to say that wisdom is even more enduring than the "dyed colors of India."

The influence of Indian textiles in the English-speaking world is revealed in such names as *calico, sash, shawl, pajama, gingham, dimity, dungaree, bandanna, chintz, khaki*—and these are only a few among the textile terms which India has exported with her fabrics.

How did she manage to exert supremacy over such a long period? This is a question requiring answer if we are to understand Indian textiles in their historical perspective.

An initial answer is to be sought in abundance and cheapness of raw materials. India is the original home of cotton, which was woven there in prehistoric times. Fragments of cotton cloth survive among the archaeological remains of Mohenjo-Daro, dating from the third millennium B.C., and even more significant is the fact that one fragment shows signs of having been dyed with madder, the use of which presupposes a knowledge of mordants. Until as late as the seventeenth century A.D., the Indians alone had mastered the complicated chemistry of cotton-dyeing, involving proper permeation of the fibres, as distinct from the mere application of pigments to the surface. This presented technical problems which did not apply to the dyeing of non-vegetable fibres such as silk and wool. Silk-weaving is mentioned in Indian texts at least as early as the third century B.C.; but the implication is that at this time only wild silks were known. There is no evidence that the cultivated silkworm reached India from China before the first centuries of our era.

Another, perhaps equally important, clue to India's traditional textile skill is the social one of caste. It would be difficult to imagine some of the extremely complicated and laborious techniques employed outside the context of a long-established caste division of labor. We use a Portuguese word *caste* for want of an alternative, but it tends to misrepresent Indian craft organization, having, as it does, other irrelevant meanings and associations. The Indian caste system, as we are here concerned with it, combines features of both tribal and guild organization. It would be difficult to imagine any craft system more calculated to encourage specialization and the accumulation of hereditary skill. In some respects, castes had functions comparable with the craft-guilds of Europe. But whereas the latter lasted only *hundreds* of years, Indian caste conventions have survived for *thousands*. Even physique was changed by so many generations of specialized craftsmanship. This was tragically shown in the nineteenth century, when tens of thousands of Indian weavers were thrown out of work by the competition of the power-loom, and found that their hands were unfit for any other manual occupation. As a result they

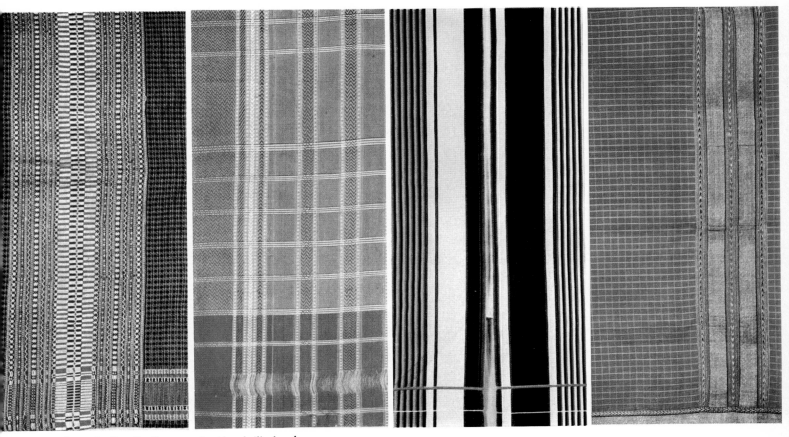

Left to right: Detail of loom-embroidered silk shawl
Sind, 20th century
The Calico Museum of Textiles, Ahmedabad

Detail of silk sari
Hyderabad, late 19th century
Collection Mrs. Sheila Bharat Ram, New Delhi

Detail of handloom striped cotton shawl
Manipur, Assam, 20th century
All India Handicrafts Board, New Delhi

Detail of handloom silk sari
Western India, 20th century
All India Handicrafts Board, New Delhi

Left: Detail of printed silk
Block printed in Assam, woven in
Bombay State. 20th century
All India Handicrafts Board, New Delhi
Right: Detail of embroidered and appliquéd canopy
Uttar Pradesh, early 20th century
Victoria and Albert Museum, London; Archer Loan Collection

starved, and their deaths are recorded in the famous minute of Governor-General Lord Bentinck which began: "The bones of cotton-weavers are bleaching the plains of India. . . ."

A convenient classification of fabrics made in India for Indian use can be made on the following basis: (1) skilled work of professional weavers and dyers who usually worked close to large market towns; (2) articles of luxury made under court patronage or in the court tradition; (3) folk-embroidery and (4) fabrics of the aboriginal tribes.

Among those in the first group are brocades, *bandanna* work or tie-and-dye, muslins and painted and printed cottons. Brocades include examples of the famous kincobs (*kimkhabs*) of Benares and Ahmedabad, woven in silk and gold and silver thread, on looms not very different from the brocade handlooms of the West. There are also *himru* brocades of mixed cotton and silk, woven primarily for Mohammedans, who were not allowed to wear garments of pure silk.

Tie-dye or *bandanna* fabrics represent one of the oldest Indian techniques. It consists in tying tightly with waxed strings portions of a silk or cotton cloth before dipping it into the dye-vat. The strings are afterwards untied, the parts which were protected remaining uncolored to form the pattern. This technique lends itself most effectively to patterns composed of all-over spots, or circles or groups of spots. Gujarat and Rajputana are the main centers of tie-dye work. Here, the cloths are known as *chunaris* and are classified according to the number of knots in the repeat. Crude tie-dye work on coarse calico comes from many parts of India, especially Assam and the Deccan.

The so-called *ikat*-technique is another kind of tie-dye. (The widespread use in textile literature of the Javanese word *ikat* must not be allowed to conceal the fact that, as far as Asia is concerned, India is probably the source of the technique.) In the making of these cloths, the warp and weft threads are dyed separately by the tie-dye process before weaving. *Ikats* are made in several parts of India; besides the well-known *patola* marriage saris of Gujarat, notable examples are the cotton shawls of Orissa and *telia rumals* of the Deccan. Traditional patterns are geometrical in kind: trellis-work, lozenges, chevrons —the special effect being the subtle merging of adjoining colors. Some of the floral scrolls and human figures sometimes appearing in nineteenth-century designs are not traditional and may be taken as a sign of decadence.

Another kind of tie-dye cloth is the *mashru* of mixed silk and cotton, in which the warp only is tie-dyed before weaving with characteristic patterns of wavy lines.

Printing and painting on cotton are the arts for which Indian textiles have been chiefly famed abroad. The distinction between *painted* and *printed* is of more than technical interest. In the *painting* of cotton, the dyes and mordants are applied freehand with a brush. Thus each design has the character of an individual drawing, with the human and sensuous touch. In printing, on the other hand, the use of wood blocks inevitably restricts the design to repeats, and only the most skilled mastery of this art can eliminate a mechanical effect. Sometimes the two techniques were combined in the making of a single cloth, a typical example being number 47.

The second classification is that of the textiles produced for the rulers and their courts, in which Persian influence is most apparent, especially in the use of a diaper: there is no evidence that it is featured at all in Indian textile design before the sixteenth century. By the middle of the seventeenth century it appears to have been completely assimilated in Indian decorative tradition.

Although the spread of Persian influence is undeniable, the term "Indo-Persian" should be applied with caution, if it is not to become meaningless. It is true that in the late sixteenth century, Persian craftsmen were encouraged to settle and to instruct Indians in the court workshops of the Mogul and Deccani rulers. As far as individual products of these workshops are concerned, the term "Indo-Persian" can often be legitimately applied. But beyond the immediate sphere of the court, Persian motives were adapted by Indian craftsmen for their own purposes and made subservient to the more earthy and dynamic qualities of Indian art as a whole.

There have been many periods in Indian history when her craftsmen have borrowed freely from the West, beginning with the Indus civilization of the third millennium B.C. and extending to the growth of Islamic architecture in India from the thirteenth century A.D. onwards. But each phase of borrowing has merely illustrated the encompassing personality of India: her extraordinary capacity for combined assimilation and invention. The influence of Persia in the decorative arts of the seventeenth and eighteenth centuries is no exception.

The third classification is the embroidery, traditionally done by women, and belonging to the villages. Styles are broadly regional, like the local traditions of folk-art to which they are related. In spite of commercialization in some areas and at different periods, the regional characteristics are distinctive: and even today, with Indian folk-traditions everywhere in decay, it is still possible to identify at centers of pilgrimage the satin-stitch *phulkari* embroideries of the punjab, chain-stitch work of Cutch and Kathiawar, cross-stitch work of Sind, and the *kantha* embroideries of Bengal. Each of these regional styles has its distinctive combinations of technique, color and design; and each has its counterpart in commercial embroidery produced for the export market.

Another type of folk fabric is derived from *alponas*—the patterns which village-women of Bengal draw in rice-paste on the threshold of their dwellings. These drawings are not ornament but symbols, and an understanding of their function helps to explain much about the forms of Indian decorative art as a whole. Briefly, *alponas* are drawings required for the enactment of rituals performed by women of the village at times of crisis. The objective may be the promotion of rain, success of the harvest, or the safety of the village against epidemic: the usual underlying idea is that when mimed in ritual, the objective is more likely to be realized. When crops are ripening, for instance, ritual is performed with the help of a drawing of a tree. This serves as a fertility symbol. The tree is drawn on the ground in white rice-paste according to established conventions of design; it then forms the center for the action of the ritual, when women sing in chorus:

> *We worship the painted mandir tree*
> *Which promises us granaries full of rice and paddy.*
> *We worship the rice-paste drawing of the mandir,*
> *Knowing that our homeland will be rich in gold and silver . . .*

These rituals are important for an understanding of the functional basis of popular art in India. They are fundamental in the living experiences of the people and reflect their whole attitude to life, giving rise to a culture rich in drama and imagination and deriving tremendous vitality from its group-character.

The folk-arts of India and the productions of primitive tribes are two worlds apart. Although folk-tradition draws on the memory of primitive ritual it has other features which presuppose a settled class-society and the coexistence of an orthodox or priestly culture.

Typical of the most primitive cultures are the weavings of the Nagas of Assam. Unlike traditional weaving in Hindu India, tribal weaving is entirely the work of women, who weave as part of their domestic duties—the true Naga housewife being expected to produce the clothing needed by her family. The loom here used is the single-heddle tension-loom of simple type, usually associated with Indonesia. The weaver sits on the ground, regulating the tension of the warps with the aid of a belt anchored around the small of the back. On the side opposite, the warps are fixed to a beam, which is attached to a wall or simply to two small stakes driven into the ground. Patterns are made partly by using differently colored warp and weft yarns, and partly by insertion of separate pieces of colored thread at intervals in the weaving—a technique which could be described as the simplest kind of brocading or loom-embroidery.

A Naga costume proclaims the wearers social position and his prowess, and is invested with an elaborate code of meaning. There are features which traditionally indicated sacrifices which the owner had performed; others which showed his success as a head-hunter in olden times.

Detail of Phulkari dress piece
Red cotton embroidered with yellow silk
Punjab, 19th century
Victoria and Albert Museum, London

Textiles

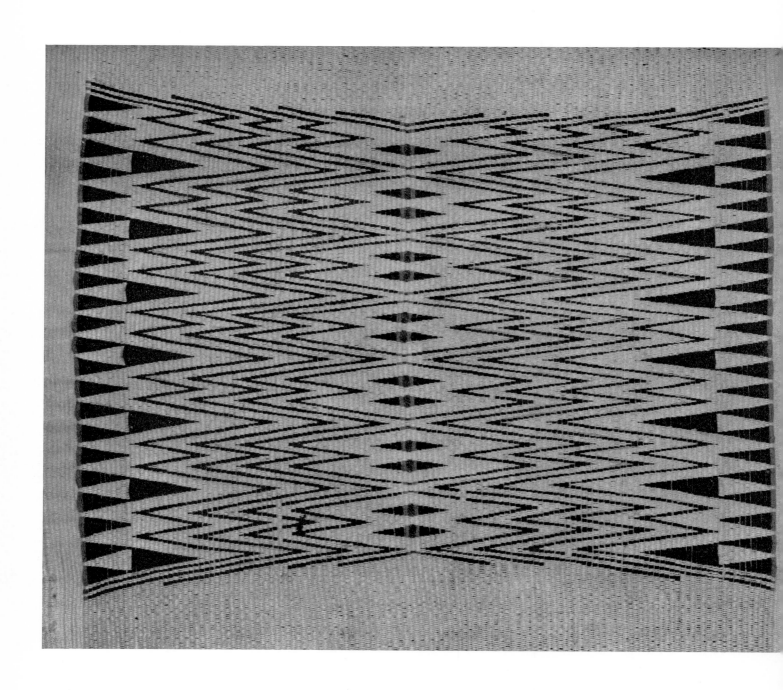

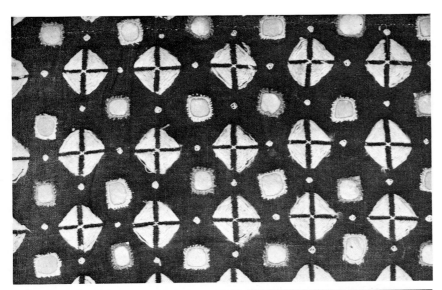

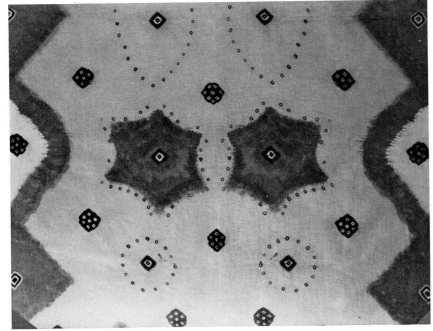

Opposite page: Detail of handloom cotton Shan bag
Black pattern on white
Assam, 20th century
Museum of Indigenous Art, New York

Above: Detail of Phulkari cotton shawl, embroidered
with yellow floss silk and ornamented with mirrors
Hissar, Punjab, 19th century
Victoria and Albert Museum, London

Below: Detail of tie-dyed peasant sari of coarse cotton
Pink, purple and yellow on natural ground
Rajasthan, 20th century
All India Handicrafts Board, New Delhi

Above: Detail of quilted cotton coat. Sand-yellow
Nepal, 20th century
The Calico Museum of Textiles, Ahmedabad

Right: Detail of an Angami Naga costume
Rust-colored and black cotton;
fringe of white wool with orange and black dangles
Assam, 20th century
The Calico Museum of Textiles, Ahmedabad

Opposite page, left: Tie-dyed satin shirt
Red dots on black ground, with gold and sequin embroidery
Cutch, middle 19th century
The Calico Museum of Textiles, Ahmedabad

Right: Detail of a brocade jacket with woven Arabic letters
Gold, red and dark blue on cream-colored ground
North India, 19th century
The Calico Museum of Textiles, Ahmedabad

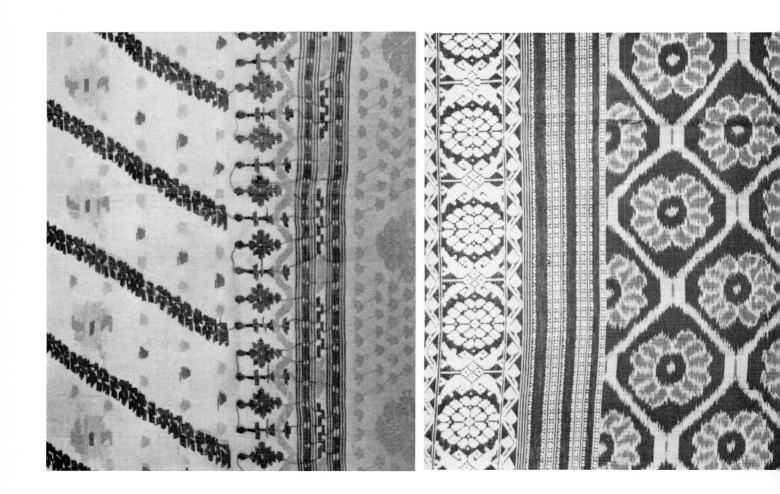

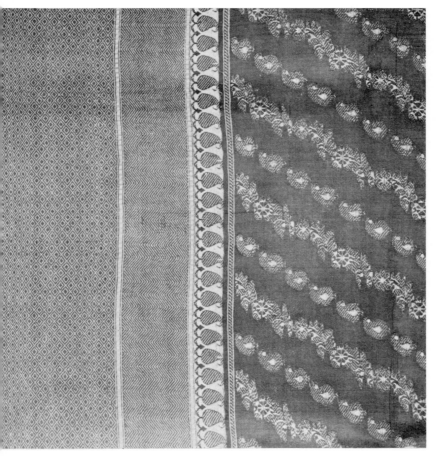

Opposite page, left: Detail of cotton tissue sari
Woven in brown, red and gold on cream-colored ground
Dacca, early 20th century
The Calico Museum of Textiles, Ahmedabad

Opposite page, right: Detail of silk sari
Red, pale yellow and white figure on dark brown;
border worked in yellow and white
Orissa, 20th century
Collection Mrs. Sheila Bharat Ram, New Delhi

This page: Copy of old silk brocade. Purple ground
with design in silver, gold and magenta
Benares, early 20th century
Collection Mrs. Sheila Bharat Ram, New Delhi

Following pages, left: Detail of satin veil, embroidered with silk
Dark blue. Central medallion set with mirrors
Cutch, 19th century
The Calico Museum of Textiles, Ahmedabad

Right: Detail of Kashmir shawl. Medallion in rose-red,
dark green and pale yellow on buff ground
Lahore, 17th century
The Heeramaneck Gallery, New York

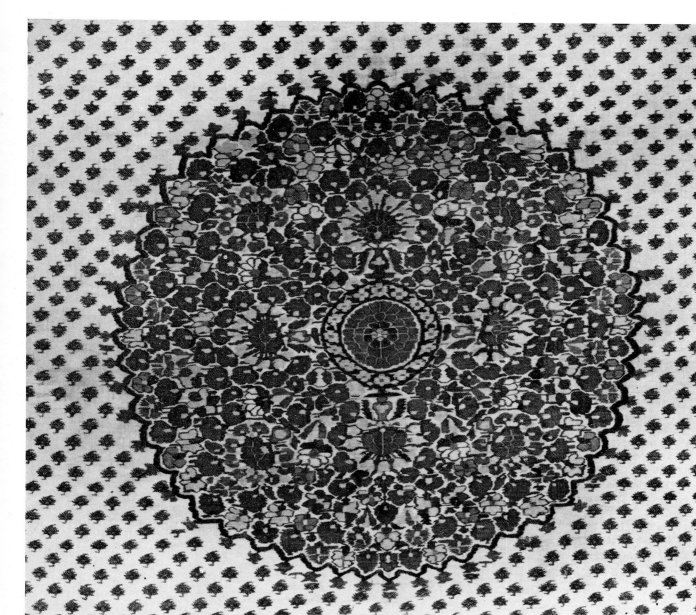

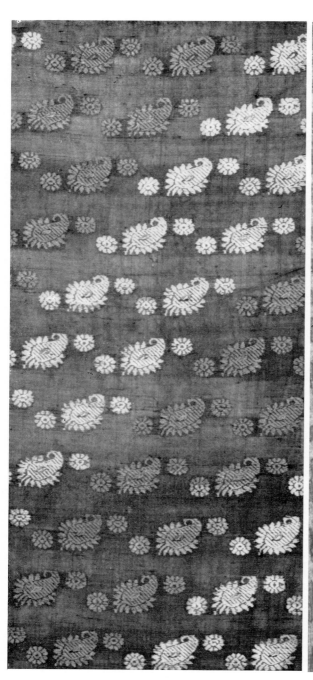

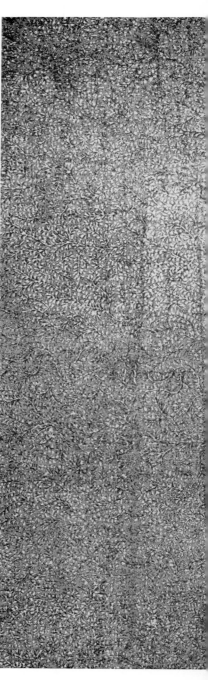

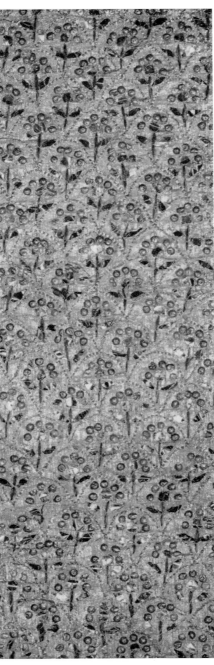

Opposite page, left: Detail of silk Baluchar sari
Red-violet ground with design in
turquoise, cerise, white and pale yellow
West Bengal, early 19th century
Collection Mrs. Sheila Bharat Ram, New Delhi

Center: Figured muslin
White figure on white ground
Dacca, 19th century
Victoria and Albert Museum, London

Right: Cotton gauze
Printed in gold and red on natural ground
17th century
Textile Museum, Washington, D.C.

This page, left: Detail of tinsel-printed shawl
Muslin gauze printed in gold,
pink and coral on natural ground
Probably of Punjab origin, late 18th century
Prince of Wales Museum of Western India, Bombay

Right: Detail of gold tissue dress piece,
embroidered with silver paillettes
and red and green tinsel
Hyderabad, Deccan, 19th century
Victoria and Albert Museum, London

Above, left: Detail of gold tissue sari, embroidered in pink, orange, blue and pale green
Chanderi, Gwalior State, late 17th century
The Heeramaneck Gallery, New York

Right: Detail of Dorakha Kashmir shawl
Dark blue ground with a unique bed-of-roses design worked in dark red, sage-green and straw-yellow
Kashmir, 18th century
Crafts Museum, New Delhi

Opposite page, left: Detail of Karupuri sari
Red and gold with figure printed in black, white and gold
Tanjore, 17th century
The Calico Museum of Textiles, Ahmedabad

Right: Detail of silk embroidered cotton sash
Late 17th century
The Metropolitan Museum of Art, New York

46

This page: Detail of cotton cummerbund. Figure stenciled
and painted in sage-green, yellow and red on cream-colored ground
Golconda, 17th century
The Heeramaneck Gallery, New York

Opposite page, left: Detail of silk brocade shawl
Border of coral, red and green flowers
against background of gold thread
Chanderi, 18th century
The Calico Museum of Textiles, Ahmedabad

Right: Detail of painted and printed cotton hanging
Late 17th century
The Metropolitan Museum of Art, New York

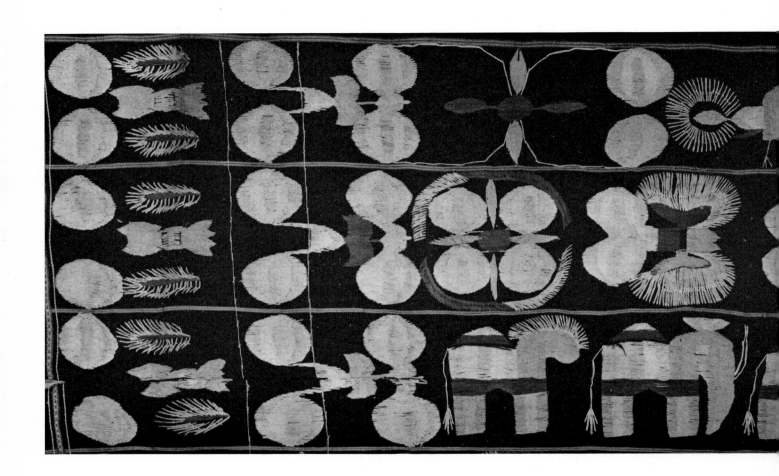

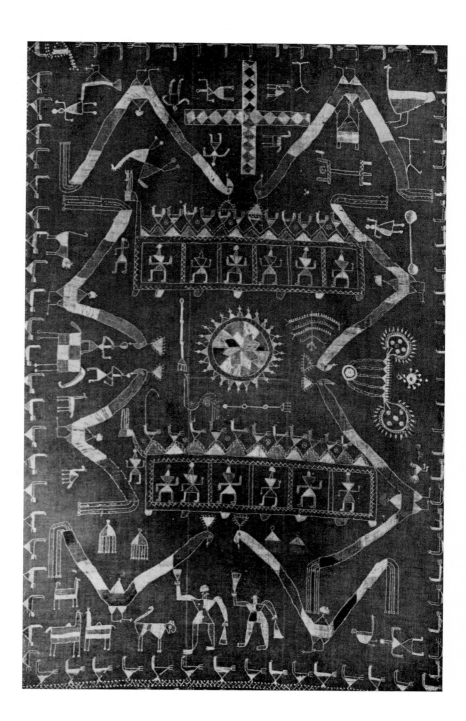

Opposite page: Detail of an Angami Naga costume
Black cotton ground with large figures
embroidered in white, brilliant yellow and orange
Assam, 20th century
The Calico Museum of Textiles, Ahmedabad

Right: Detail of curtain. Dark-green cotton
embroidered in saffron, red and white silk
Kangra or Chamba, early 19th century
Victoria and Albert Museum, London

Left, above: Fragment of carpet
Design of mythological beasts in cream-color,
peacock blue, ochre and pale orange on dark-red ground
Textile Museum, Washington, D.C.

Below: Fragment of Dari carpet
Design motif of mythological beast in ochre,
dark blue and white on dark-red ground
Mogul, 17th century
The Calico Museum of Textiles, Ahmedabad

Opposite page: Detail of cotton coverlet
Embroidered with scenes from the Ramayana
in colored silks and tinsel
Chamba, 18th century
The Metropolitan Museum of Art, New York

Above: Fragment of indigo resist-dyed cotton
Indigo ground with figure in white and light blue
Found in a 12th-century tomb at Fostat, Egypt
Textile Museum, Washington, D.C.

Opposite page: Detail of Baluchar silk sari
Crimson background with figure in peacock blue and white
Bengal, 19th century
Collection Mrs. Sheila Bharat Ram, New Delhi

Opposite page: Detail of Kangra coverlet
embroidered in earth green, ochre,
dark blue and red on natural ground
Lent anonymously to the Textile Museum, Washington, D.C.

This page, above: Fragment with design of mythological marine figures
printed in dark red, olive green,
violet and ochre on muted pink background
Textile Museum, Washington, D.C.

Below: Detail of silk hanging
satin tissue with yellow brocaded figures on dark-red ground
Rajputana, Western India, early 17th century
The Heeramaneck Gallery, New York

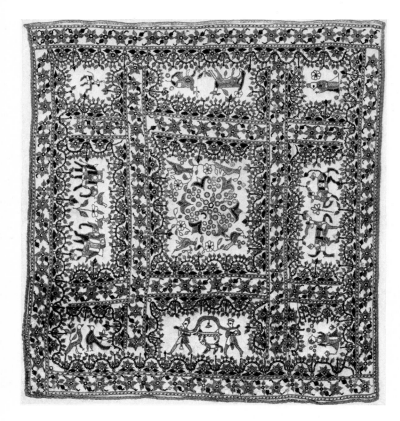

Left: Coverlet. Embroidered in red, turquoise
and black silk on golden-yellow satin, and set with mirrors
Cutch, 19th century
Victoria and Albert Museum, London

Opposite page: Detail of painted cotton hanging
Design represents milkmaids in a flowering forest;
gold and silver on black ground
Rappritana, 18th century
The Heeramaneck Gallery, New York

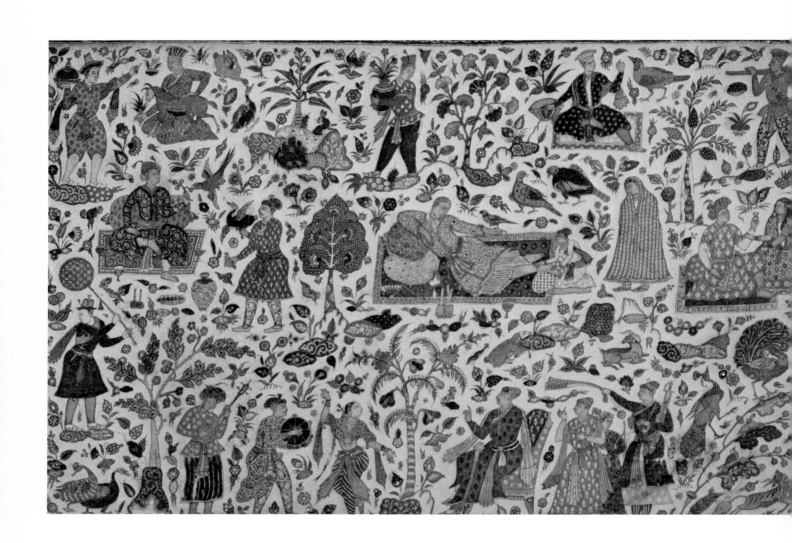

Opposite page: Detail of cushion cover
Dyed and painted cotton
Mogul, about 1615–1640
The Metropolitan Museum of Art, New York

This page, above: Detail of temple hanging. Printed cotton
South India, 19th century
Victoria and Albert Museum, London

Below: Detail of quilted cotton Kantha
Design depicts festival performances amidst symbols.
Mid-19th century
Private collection

Cotton temple hanging; hand-painted in dye colors
with illustrations from the Ramayana. Design in dark red,
black and ochre, with central figures in ink blue
North Arcot, Madras, 19th century
Victoria and Albert Museum, London

Above: Cover of a knuckle-pad originally attached to shield
Embroidered in dark purple,
rose and yellow silk on buff-colored cotton ground
Jaipur, Rajputana, 18th century
Victoria and Albert Museum, London

Below: Necklace of gold beads with detail of silk embroidered Kantha

Emblem for standard
Ornamental calligraphy
in gilt copper openwork. Height: 13¾"
Mogul, Delhi, 17th century
Victoria and Albert Museum, London

Ornaments

Top to bottom: Gold enamel pendant. Depicts Radha with garland and Krishna with flute in Brndaban Forest. 1 x 1¼″
Jaipur, 17th–18th century
Museum of Fine Arts, Boston

Gold enamel pendant. Depicts Krishna with two attendants; white, blue, lavender, green and red enamel on gold ground. 1⅞ x 1½″
16th or 17th century
The Cleveland Museum of Art

Pendant of gold and precious stones
Depicts ten avatars of Vishnu: colored enamels, rubies, emeralds and diamonds. 1¾ x 1⅞″
Jaipur, 16th century
Museum of Fine Arts, Boston

Gold enamel pendant. Depicts footprints of the Lord. 1¼ x 1⅜″
Jaipur, 17th–18th century
Museum of Fine Arts, Boston

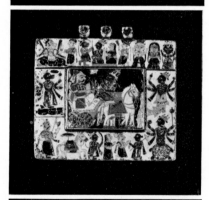

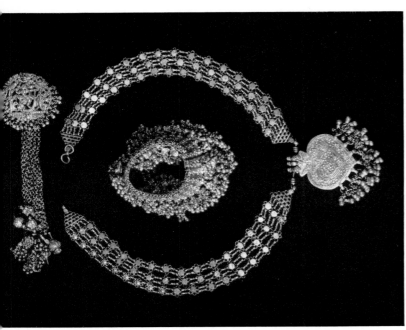

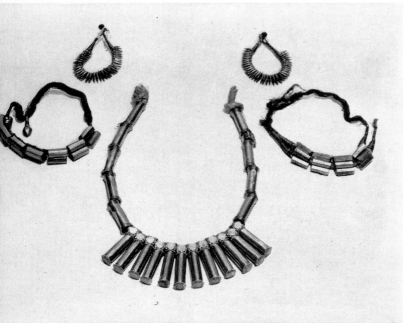

Left: Silver chatelaine
Madras Province, 19th century
The Metropolitan Museum of Art, New York

Silver anklet
Ajmir, 19th century
Victoria and Albert Museum, London

Silver necklet
Madras Province, 19th century
The Metropolitan Museum of Art, New York

Below, top: Pair of gilt metal bracelets
Bengal, c. 1870

Below, left: Gilt metal bracelet, ends formed of twisted silver thread
Delhi, c. 1870

Below, right: Gilt metal bracelet
Bengal, c. 1870

Below, center: Necklace of cylindrical gold ornaments
Bengal, 19th century
All from the Victoria and Albert Museum, London

One of a pair of openwork silver bangles
Bombay, 19th century
Victoria and Albert Museum, London

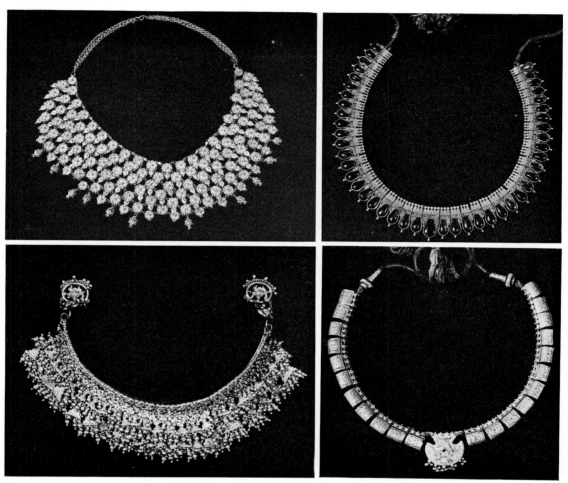

Above, left: Gold necklace; consisting of small plaques,
chased and ornamented with granulated work and joined by gold links
Mohammedan style, Bombay, 19th century

Above, right: Gold headband
set with pear-shaped cabochon emeralds and rubies
South India, 17th century

Below, left: Gold forehead ornament for a bridegroom
Lucknow, Oudh, 19th century
All from the Victoria and Albert Museum, London

Below, right: Gold necklace made of amulet boxes
18th or 19th century
The Metropolitan Museum of Art, New York

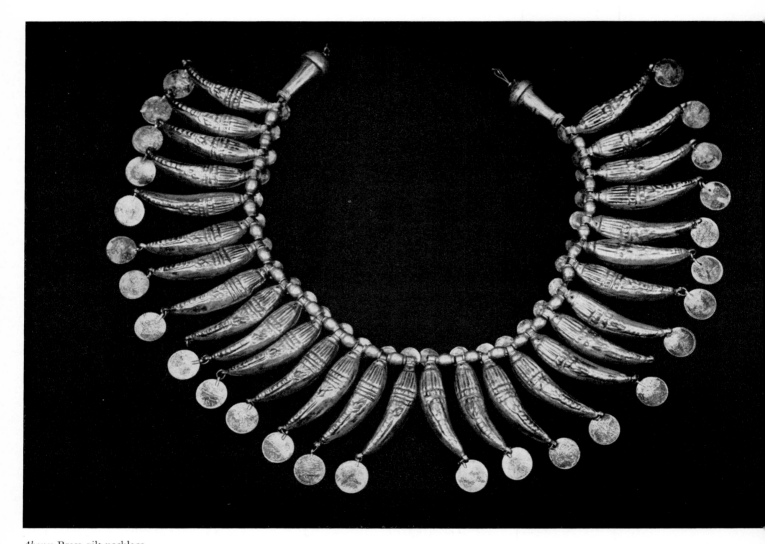

Above: Brass-gilt necklace,
consisting of pendants with silver-gilt coins
Sinhalese, 19th century
Victoria and Albert Museum, London

Opposite page: Necklace for a little girl
19th century
Victoria and Albert Museum, London

70

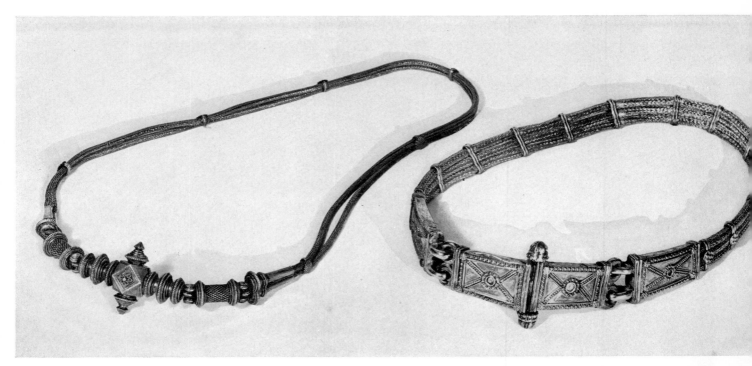

Above, left: Silver belt; consisting of two flexible chains
united by narrow bands
Deccan, 19th century
Chicago Natural History Museum

Right: Silver belt; consisting of three chains of plaited wire
with two plaques at each end
Poona, 19th century
Victoria and Albert Museum, London

Opposite page: left to right: Pair of silver armlets
Dera Ismail Kahn, Punjab, 19th century

One of a pair of chased silver anklets
Madras, 19th century (c. 1872)

One of a pair of silver bracelets,
in the form of a dragon's neck with two heads
Sind, 19th century
All from the Victoria and Albert Museum, London

Above, left to right: Silver bracelet
20th century
All India Handicrafts Board, New Delhi

One of a pair of silver-plated brass anklets
19th century
The Metropolitan Museum of Art, New York

White metal anklet, cast by the cire-perdue process
Bengal, 19th century
Victoria and Albert Museum, London

Silver anklet
Bombay, 19th century
Chicago Natural History Museum

Below, left to right: One of a pair of white metal anklets
Bombay, c. 1872

Gold bracelet. Mogul pattern
Bombay, 19th century
Both from the Victoria and Albert Museum, London

Gold armlet, set with diamonds and rubies
18th or 19th century
The Metropolitan Museum of Art, New York

White metal anklet
Mysore, 19th century
Victoria and Albert Museum, London

Brass chain for hanging seat or bed. Height: 6'
Kathiawar, 19th century
Victoria and Albert Museum, London

Opposite page: Dome-shaped tea basket. Height: c. 16"
Assam, 20th century
All India Handicrafts Board, New Delhi

Above: Jade dish in form of a leaf. Length: 5½″
Mogul, 17th century
Victoria and Albert Museum, London

Opposite page: left to right: Jade jar; overlaid with gold and precious stones. Height: 4½″
Mogul, 17th century
Victoria and Albert Museum, London

Deep jade bowl. Height: 5¼″
Mogul, 17th century
The Heeramaneck Gallery, New York

Green jade wine cup. Formerly two-handled, with incised inscriptions
inlaid with white cement.
Made for the Mogul Emperor Jahangir *(1605–1627 A.D.).* Height: 1½″
Mogul, dated 1022 A.H. (1613 A.D.)
Victoria and Albert Museum, London

78

Below: Carved soapstone powder boxes. Height: c. 3 to 3½″
Bengal, 20th century
All India Handicrafts Board, New Delhi

Right, above: Carved soapstone powder box. Height: 5½″
Allahbad, 19th century
Victoria and Albert Museum, London

Right, below: Tray; made of grains of rice stitched together
and interwoven with gold tinsel. Diameter: 8¼″
20th century
All India Handicrafts Board, New Delhi

Opposite page: Brass bowl. Height: 6″
Benares, 19th century
Prince of Wales Museum of Western India, Bombay

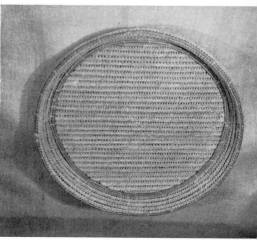

Above: left to right: Brass bowl and cover. Height: 9½″. *19th century*
Brass bowl, with applied wire decoration. Height: 3¾″
Both from the Victoria and Albert Museum, London
Brass bowl. Height: 6″. *Benares, 19th century.* Prince of Wales Museum of Western India, Bombay
Brass bowl. Height: c. 4″. *Orissa, 20th century.* Crafts Museum, New Delhi
Copper holy water bowl and dipper. *20th century.* All India Handicrafts Board, New Delhi
Brass votive candelabra; depicting Krishna supported on a circular stand,
surrounded by four milkmaids. Height: 7⅛″. *Bengal, 19th century.* Private collection

Opposite page: left to right: Chased bronze spice box in shape of fish. Length: 17¾″. *19th century*
Brass spice box, with design motif of female faces. Height: 9½″. *19th century*
Silver spice box. Enameled and jeweled with flower and bird motifs. Height: 3½″. *Lucknow, Oudh, c. 1700*
Cast brass perfume holder, with receptacles for pulverized sandalwood and other powders. Height: 5⅝″
All from the Victoria and Albert Museum, London

Above: Palanquin or shamiyana pole ends; silver gilt with punched
and raised decoration, in the form of tiger heads. Height: c. 8″
Delhi, 19th century
Victoria and Albert Museum, London

Opposite page: "Tippu's Tiger." Wood, containing mechanical organ
to produce animal and human sounds. Length: 7′
Seringapatam, Mysore, c. 1790
Victoria and Albert Museum, London

Above, left: Copper mask, representing Nandi, the bull. Height: 11″
South India, 19th century

Right: Cast bronze mask of a tusked boar. Height: 11″
From a Vaishnara temple, Madras, 19th century
Both from the Victoria and Albert Museum, London

Opposite page, left: Iron cat. Height: 2½″
Sialkot, Punjab, 18th century
Prince of Wales Museum of Western India, Bombay

Right: Bidri fish-shaped boxes. Silver on iron. Length: 9½″ and 6″
Hyderabad, Deccan, 18th century
Prince of Wales Museum of Western India, Bombay

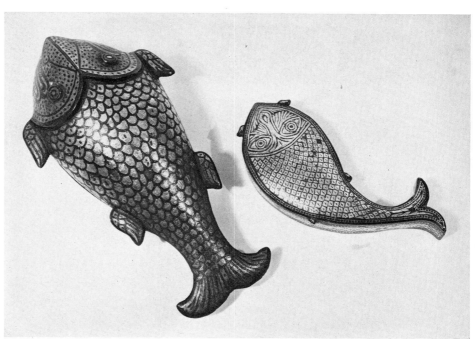

Opposite page: left to right: Carved wood votive figure
Tirupati, Orissa, 20th century
All India Handicrafts Board, New Delhi

Painted pith sculpture; ritual image
20th century
All India Handicrafts Board, New Delhi

Painted wood figurine. Height: 11⅜"
Orissa, 20th century

Painted wood shrine. Height: c. 17"
Orissa, 20th century
Both collection Alexander Girard, Santa Fé, New Mexico

This page: Brass temple lamp. Made up of 3 tiers of oil burners,
each surmounted by a peacock. Height: 5′ 1″
19th century?
Victoria and Albert Museum, London

Group of toys: *Left to right:*

Hunting group, consisting of chief and six attendants; brass.

Brass partridge. *Both Madras, 19th century*

Painted grotesque animal. *Surat*

Two-headed horned animal; cast brass. *Central Provinces, 19th century*

Painted tiger. *Surat, 19th century*

Brass pea hen. *Madras, 19th century*

Painted monkey. *Surat, 19th century*

Brass deer with wire horns. *Madras, 19th century*

Height: 3½″ to 8″. All from the Victoria and Albert Museum, London

Opposite page: Group of clay tribal figurines of Kali Paraj people. Height: 2½″ to 12″. *Bombay State, 20th century*

All collection Alexander Girard, Santa Fé, New Mexico

Toy boat with figures; carved and painted ivory. Length: 37″
Rajput-Mogul, 18th century
The Heeramaneck Gallery, New York

Selected Bibliography of Indian Textiles

BY JOHN IRWIN

General Works

All India Handicrafts Board. *Handicrafts of India.* Government of India, New Delhi, 1955.

Baden-Powell, B. H. *Handbook of the manufactures and arts of the Punjab,* comprising vol. II of the *Handbook of the economic products of the Punjab,* Lahore, 1872.

Birdwood, G. C. M. *The industrial arts of India,* 2 vols., London, 1880.

Codrington, K. de B. *The minor arts of India.* An essay included in the symposium *Indian art,* edited by Sir Richard Winstedt, London, 1947.

Coomaraswamy, A. K. *Arts and crafts of India and Ceylon,* Edinburgh, 1913.

Irwin, John. *Indian textiles.* An essay included in *The art of India and Pakistan: commemorative catalogue of the exhibition held at the Royal Academy of Arts, London, 1947–8,* edited by Sir Leigh Ashton, London, 1950.

Jayakar, Pupul. *Indian printed textiles.* All India Handicrafts Board, Government of India, published by Marg Publications, Bombay, 1954.

Mukharji, T. N. *Art-manufactures of India,* Calcutta, 1888.

Watson, John Forbes. *Textile manufactures and costumes of the people of India,* London, 1866.

> *Collection of specimens and illustrations of the textile manufactures of India,* 4 vols. fol., 13 vols. 4to, London, 1873–80.

Watt, (Sir) George. *Indian art at Delhi.* Official catalogue of the Delhi Exhibition, 1902–3, London, 1904.

Costume

Chandra, Dr. Moti. *History of Indian costume from 1st–4th century A.D.,* Journal of Indian Society of Oriental Art, Calcutta, vol. 8, 1940.

Ghurye, G. S. *Indian costume,* Bombay, 1950.

Leix, A. *Periods of civilization and the development of dress in India,* Ciba Review, Basle, no. 36, 1940.

> *Costumes of the people of India,* Ciba Review, Basle, no. 36, 1940.

Watson, John Forbes and Kaye, J. W. *The people of India. A series of photographic illustrations, with descriptive letterpress, of the races and tribes of Hindustan.* . . . 8 vols., London, 1868–72.

Williamson, T. *The costumes and customs of modern India.* With drawings by C. Doyley. London, 1813.

Ancient and Medieval Textiles

Codrington, K. de B. *Culture of medieval India as illustrated by the Ajanta Frescoes,* The Indian Antiquary, Bombay, vol. LIX, 1930.

Geijer, Agnes. *Some evidence of Indo-European cotton trade in pre-Mughal times,* Journal of Indian Textile History, Ahmedabad, no. 1, 1955.

Pfister, R. *Tissus imprimées de Fostat et l'Hindustan,* Paris, 1938.

Ray, Joges Chandra. *Textile industry in ancient India,* Journal of Bihar and Orissa Research Society, vol. III, pt. 2, 1917.

16th to 18th Century Textiles

D'Allemagne, Henry-René. *La toile imprimée et les indiennes de traite,* 2 vols., Paris, 1942.

Baker, G. P. *Cotton painting and printing in the East Indies,* 2 vols., London, 1920.

Brett, K. B. *An English source of Indian chintz design,* Journal of Indian Textile History, Ahmedabad, no. 1, 1955.

Hadaway, W. S. *Cotton painting and printing in the Madras Presidency,* Madras, 1917.

Irwin, John. *Indo-Portuguese embroideries of Bengal,* Arts and Letters: Journal of Royal India, Pakistan and Ceylon Society, London, vol. XXVI, no. 2, 1952.

> *The commercial embroidery of Gujerat in the 17th Century,* Journal of Indian Society of Oriental Art, Calcutta, vol. XVII, 1949 (issued 1953).

> *A 17th-century painted calico from the Coromandel Coast,* The Connoisseur, London, vol. 132, 1955.

> *Origins of the "Oriental Style" in English decorative art,* Burlington Magazine, London, vol. 97, 1955.

> *Indian textile trade in the 17th century,* Journal of Indian Textile History, Ahmedabad, no. 1, 1955.

Mendonça, Maria José. *Alguns tipos de colchas Indo-Portuguesas na colecção do Museu Nacional de Arte Antiga,* Museum bulletin (Lisbon), vol. 2, 1951.

Moreland, W. H. *Indian exports of cotton goods in the 17th century,* Indian Journal of Economics, Allahabad, 1925.

Rieftstahl, R. M. *Persian and Indian textiles, from 16th to early 19th century,* New York, 1923.

Slomann, Wilhelm. *Bizarre designs in silks,* Copenhagen, 1953.

19th Century Textiles

(A) COTTON FABRICS

Anonymous. *Descriptive and historical account of the cotton manufactures of Dacca,* London, 1851.

Bunt, C. G. E. *The technique of Indian muslins,* Textile World, New York, vol. 63, 1923.

Enthoven, R. E. *Cotton fabrics of Bombay Presidency.* Journal of Indian Art and Industry, London, vol. 10, 1909.

Francis, E. B. *Monograph on cotton manufacture in the Punjab,* Punjab Government Press, 1884.

Havell, E. B. *Printed cotton industry of India,* Journal of Indian Art, London, vol. 2, no. 19, 1888.

" *The industries of Madras,* Journal of Indian Art, London, vol. 3, no. 27, 1890.

Jayakar, Pupul. *Indian printed textiles.* All India Handicrafts Board, Government of India, Marg Publications, Bombay, 1954.

Kipling, J. L. *Punjab cotton prints,* Journal of Indian Art, London, vol. I, no. 14, 1886.

" *Plant drawings from an Indian cotton-painter's pattern book,* Studio Magazine, London, vol. 18, 1910.

Lewis, A. B. *Blockprints from India for textiles,* Field Museum of Natural History, Chicago, Anthropology Design Series, 1924.

Ravenshaw, C. W. *Cloth Stamping and dyeing* (in Beawar), Journal of Indian Art, London, vol. 2, no. 17, 1888.

Sammam, H. *The cotton fabrics of Assam,* Journal of Indian Art and Industry, London, vol. 10, 1903.

Silberrad, C. A. *Cotton fabrics of the N.W. Provinces and Oudh,* Journal of Indian Art and Industry, London, vol. 10, 1904.

Thurston, Edgar. *The cotton fabric industry of the Madras Presidency,* Journal of Indian Art, vol. 7, no. 59, 1897.

Venkataraman. *The handloom industry in South India,* Dept. of Economics, Madras University, 1940.

(B) SILK FABRICS

Allen, B. C. *Monograph on the silk cloths of Assam,* Calcutta, 1899.

Dewar, F. *Silk fabrics of the Central Provinces,* Journal of Indian Art, London, vol. X, 1903.

Edwards, S. M. *Silk fabrics of Bombay Presidency,* Journal of Indian Art and Industry, London, vol. X, 1909.

Gulati, A. N. *The Patolu of Gujarat,* Museum Association of India, Bombay, 1951.

Hailey, W. *Silk Industry in the Punjab,* Journal of Indian Art and Industry, vol. 10, 1904.

Mookerji, Nitya Gopal. *The silk industries of Bengal,* Journal of Indian Art, London, vol. 5, no. 38, 1894.

Steel, F. A. *Monograph on silk industry in the Punjab,* Punjab Government Press, Lahore, 1887.

Trivedi, A. B. *The silk weaving industry of Surat,* Bombay University Journal, vol. X (N.S.), 1942.

Yusuf Ali, A. *Monograph on silk fabrics produced in the N.W. Provinces and Oudh,* Allahabad, 1900.

(C) WOOLEN FABRICS

Brandon, B. *Woollen fabrics of Bombay Presidency,* Journal of Indian Art and Industry, London, vol. 10, 1903.

Irwin, John. *Shawls: A study in Indo-European exchange,* Victoria and Albert Museum Monograph, London, 1955.

Johnstone, D. C. *Monograph on woollen manufactures of the Punjab,* Punjab Government Press, 1886.

Rey, J. *Études pour servir à l'histoire des châles,* Paris, 1823.

(D) EMBROIDERY

Dongerkery, Kamala S. *The romance of Indian embroidery,* Bombay, 1951.

Ganguli, Kalyan Kumar. *Chambā Rumāl,* Journal of Indian Society of Oriental Art, Calcutta, vol. XI, 1943.

Irwin, John. *Indian embroidery,* Victoria and Albert Museum, Large Picture Book No. 7, London, 1951.

Kramrisch, Stella. *Kanthā,* Journal of Indian Society of Oriental Art, Calcutta, vol. 7, 1939.

Steel, Mrs. F. A. *Phulkari work in the Punjab,* Journal of Indian Art, London, vol. 2, no. 24, 1888.

This book has been designed by Norman Ives and printed in February 1956 for the Trustees of the Museum of Modern Art by Case, Lockwood and Brainard, Hartford, Connecticut. The color plates were manufactured and printed by Brüder Hartmann, West Berlin, Germany.